Movement of The Way
Tenuat HaDerekh

Sacred Movement & Breath
with the Living Letters of Light

*A healing practice for body, soul, and spirit
rooted in Scripture, resonance, and faith.*

Chaplain Shawnna Schmidt

Tenuat HaDerekh
Sacred Movement & Breath with the Living Letters of Light

Copyright © Chaplain Shawnna Schmidt 2026
Images and text Copyright © Chaplain Shawnna Schmidt
Photos used with permission
Editor Aryrejin El
Interior Design S.C. Schmidt
Cover Design S.C. Schmidt
Shomer Press Publishing
All Rights Reserved
No part of this work may be reproduced or stored using any means mechanical, electric or print without written consent of the Copyright holder.
ISBN paperback 9798988935094

Tenuat HaDerekh — Movement of the Way
A sacred practice of breath, embodiment, and return
© Chaplain Shawnna Schmidt

The Symbol of Aleph (On the cover.)
The emblem at the heart of this book bears the Hebrew letter Aleph (א), the first letter of the Aleph-Bet and the letter of beginning, breath, and presence.

Aleph has no sound of its own; it is formed by breath alone, reminding us that before prayer had words, it had breath. In Hebrew understanding, Aleph is composed of heaven above and earth below, joined by a diagonal line, the way that connects them. It is the letter of integration: spirit and body, heaven and earth, Word and flesh.

Enclosed within a circle of wholeness and covenant, Aleph here is rendered in a form that subtly resembles a human body standing, listening, and aligned. This symbol proclaims the heart of HaDerekh: that the body is a sacred vessel, movement is prayer, and The Way begins in stillness, breath, and attentive presence before God.

#MovementOfTheWay

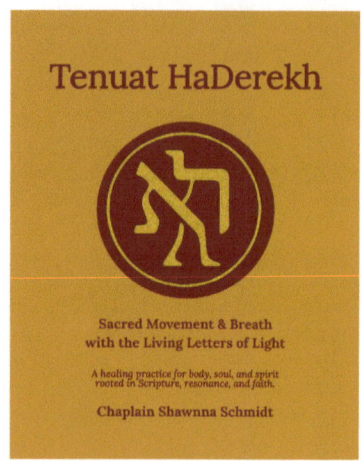

IMPORTANT NOTICE & PRACTICE DISCLAIMER

Welcome

Tenuat HaDerekh (Movement of The Way) is a gentle, spiritually rooted movement and breath practice inspired by Scripture, embodied prayer, and mindful awareness. This practice is invitational, adaptive, and designed to honor the body as a sacred vessel. This is not exercise, nor is it performance. It is prayer made visible.

Please Read Before Participating

Tenuat HaDerekh (Movement of The Way) is a spiritual movement and breath practice rooted in Scripture, embodied prayer, and gentle somatic awareness. It is designed to support reflection, grounding, worship, and personal awareness, not to diagnose, treat, or cure any medical or psychological condition.

Personal Responsibility

Assumption of Risk & Release of Liability

By engaging in this practice, you acknowledge and agree that:

- You are participating voluntarily
- You take responsibility for your own physical, emotional, and spiritual wellbeing
- You will seek appropriate professional care when needed
- You release the author, editor, instructor, facilitators, and hosts from any liability for injury, loss, or damages, including but not limited to those arising from participation
- You agree not to hold any of the above parties responsible for outcomes resulting from your voluntary participation

Spiritual Orientation

This practice is offered from a Messianic faith foundation, rooted in Scripture and The Way of Yeshua (Jesus). Participation does not require theological agreement — only respect for the spiritual framework in which it is presented.

Not Medical Advice

This practice is not a substitute for medical care, physical therapy, mental health treatment, or professional supervision. No medical or therapeutic claims are made, expressed or implied. The author, editor, and publishers are not responsible for injuries, discomfort, or adverse effects that may occur during or after participation. Always consult a qualified healthcare provider before beginning any movement, breath, or wellness practice, especially if you are pregnant, recovering from injury or surgery, living with chronic illness, neurological conditions, heart conditions, or mobility limitations.

Honor Your Body

You are encouraged to:
- Move slowly and gently
- Modify, adapt, or skip any posture
- Rest whenever needed
- Stop immediately if anything causes pain, dizziness, distress, or discomfort
- Pain is not a spiritual requirement.
- Stillness is as valid as movement.
- Listening to your body is an act of wisdom.

Adaptive & Inclusive Practice

All postures in Tenuat HaDerekh may be practiced seated, supported, or visualized. There is no "correct" expression, only an honest one. Choosing rest, stillness, or observation is fully participating.

Final Blessing

May this practice be a place of peace, not pressure.
May it restore, not strain.
May it guide you gently, always toward life.

Participants are encouraged to honor their own physical limits and to modify or rest at any time.

HaDerekh
Movement of the Way,
The Living Letters

HaDerekh, The Way is a breath-led, body-based spiritual practice rooted in the Hebrew letters as living forms. It invites readers into embodied prayer through gentle movement, sacred posture, and attentive breath. Not as performance, but as presence.

Drawing from Scripture, Hebrew thought, and the embodied ministry of Yeshua, this book reclaims the body as a sacred vessel, a place where prayer is lived, not merely spoken. Each letter becomes an invitation to listen, align, and move with intention, allowing faith to be carried not only in belief, but in the body itself.

Designed for personal devotion, group practice, and teaching settings, HaDerekh offers adaptive postures, theological reflection, and contemplative guidance accessible to all bodies and abilities. This is not exercise, nor is it performance. It is prayer made visible.

Silence is honored. Stillness is welcomed. Movement becomes a form of remembering. This book is not meant to be rushed. It is meant to be walked. Because before prayer had words, it had breath. And the body already knows the way.

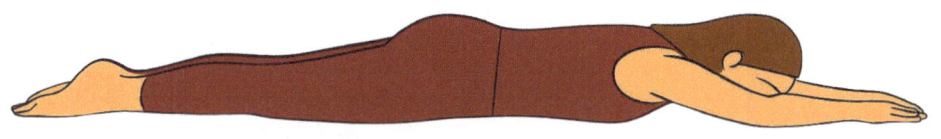

Dedication

For my daughters
May your journey be lit with
the fire of faith.
May your body remember the
rhythm of heaven.
May your steps be steady,
your breath full of praise,
and your soul always drawn to
His Way
the Way of love, of light, of life.

Love Mom

Table Of Contents

Movement of The Way
הַדֶּרֶךְ (HaDerekh)
A Living Path of Embodied Faithe

Dedication
I Am The Way : Logos & Living Word
A Word Study
Opening Blessing / Invocation
Glossary of Terms
The Way of the Living Letter
What Is Tenuat HaDerekh? (Movement of The Way)
What Makes This Practice Unique
Foundations & Worship
How to Use This Book
Guidance for Teachers & Facilitators
Foundations
The Body as Sacred Text
Breath as Ruach (The Living Breath)
Movement as Prayer
Adaptation, Accessibility, and Embodied Safety
The Hebrew Letter Movements (Aleph–Tav)
Each Letter Includes:
• Posture (Standing + Adaptive)
• Breath Instruction
• Scripture
• Reflection Phrase

The Hebrew Letters

Aleph (א)
Bet (ב)
Gimel (ג)
Dalet (ד)
Hey (ה)
Vav (ו)
Zayin (ז)
Chet (ח)
Tet (ט)
Yod (י)
Kaf / Kaf Sofit (כ / ך)
Lamed (ל)
Mem / Mem Sofit (מ / ם)
Nun / Nun Sofit (נ / ן)
Samekh (ס)
Ayin (ע)
Pei / Pei Sofit (פ / ף)
Tzadei / Tzadei Sofit (צ / ץ)
Qof (ק)
Resh (ר)
Shin (ש)
Tav (ת)

The Sacred Flow: Aleph-Tav Integration
Movement of The Way: The Sacred Flow
Teaching the Flow in Group Settings
Closings & Integration
Short Closing Blessing (Class Ending)
Spoken Closing (Teacher-Led)
Hebrew-Inflected Closing (Aleph-Tav)
Sealed in The Way — Final Blessing
Reference & Sup port
Living Letters Index (Letter • Meaning • Body Focus • Breath Theme)

A Note of Compassion: From My Heart to Yours
A personal message from Chaplain Shawnna

This practice was born not from a place of physical perfection, but from a journey of deep restorative need. My own walk with "The Way" was forged through decades of searching for tools to help my loved ones—including my son, whose journey through a failed heart repair taught me that the spirit can move even when the body is weary.

I know what it is to sit beside a bed or a wheelchair and long for a way to pray that involves more than just words. I know the beauty of a "mixed-ability" circle where every breath is a victory.

If you are coming to these pages with a body that feels broken, a heart that feels heavy, or a physical frame that moves differently than the images on the page, please know: You are not an outsider to this practice. You are the very reason it was created.

The Holy Spirit does not rush the body; He rests upon it. Whether you move through the full Aleph-Tav flow or simply rest in the "Silent Breath" of the Aleph, you are walking The Way. Your vessel is sacred, your limitations are seen with love, and your presence here is a gift.

May you move in grace, rest in mercy, and breathe in peace. Shalom

I am the Path that leads you Home.
I am the Truth that sets you free.
I am the Life that breathes eternity.
No one comes to the Father's heart
but by walking the Way I Am.

John 14:6

אֲנִי הַדֶּרֶךְ וְהָאֱמֶת וְהַחַיִּים; אִישׁ לֹא-יָבוֹא אֶל-הָאָב, אֶלָּא דַרְכִּי

Ani ha-Derekh, ve-ha-Emet, ve-ha-Chayim; ish lo yavo el ha-Av, ella darki

**I am the Way, the Truth, and the Life.
No one comes to the Father except through Me.**

אֲנִי הַדֶּרֶךְ

- <u>Ani</u> (אֲנִי) = I am
- <u>HaDerekh</u> (הַדֶּרֶךְ) = the Way / the Path / the Road

Linguistic & Biblical Context

- The Hebrew word דֶּרֶךְ <u>derekh</u> appears hundreds of times in the Hebrew Bible<u>Tanakh</u> to mean "way," "path," "manner," or even "lifestyle."
    - Psalm 119:105 "Your word is a lamp to my feet and a <u>derekh</u> to my path."
    - Isaiah 30:21 "This is the <u>derekh</u>, walk in it..."
- In John 14:6, Yeshua (Jesus) says: "I am the way, the truth, and the life."
- Likely spoken in Aramaic: <u>Ana orḥa, u-sharara, u-ḥayyeh</u>
- In Hebrew: <u>Ani HaDerekh, VeHaEmet, VeHaChayim</u>

Spiritual Significance

- <u>Derekh</u> in Hebrew is not just a direction, it implies an entire manner of being.
- When Yeshua says "I am the <u>Derekh</u>", He is:
    - Declaring Himself the path to the Father
    - The embodiment of Torah lived out
    - The model of *halakhah* (how one walks)
    - The restoration of the ancient path (Jeremiah 6:16)

Core Scripture - John 14:6

<u>Ani HaDerekh</u> - I Am The Way - אֲנִי הַדֶּרֶךְ וְהָאֱמֶת וְהַחַיִּים

<u>Ani ha-Derekh, ve-ha-Emet, ve-ha-Chayim</u>

I am the Way, the Truth, and the Life.
No one comes to the Father except through Me.

Hebrew Word Breakdown:

Hebrew Word	Hebrew Script	Pronunciation	Embodied Sense
Ani	אֲנִי	AH-nee	Presence; identity; being
HaDerekh	הַדֶּרֶךְ	hah-DEH-rekh	Walking; posture; lived faith
HaEmet	הָאֱמֶת	hah-EH-met	Alignment; integrity; balance
HaChayim	הַחַיִּים	hah-kha-YEEM	Breath; movement; renewal

Note: In Hebrew thought, these words describe not abstract ideas,
but ways of being lived through the body.
<u>HaDerekh</u> is not merely a direction but a manner of walking.
Ha<u>Emet</u> is not opinion, it is stability and faithfulness.
Ha<u>Chayim</u> is not survival, it is animated life breathed by God.

In Aramaic (Yeshua's likely spoken tongue):
Ana orḥa, u-sharara, u-ḥayyeh

May this Way bless
many bodies,
across many years,
in quiet rooms
and open fields,
long after the noise
of this age fades.
May it always remain gentle.
May it always remain free.

Glossary

HaDerekh (הַדֶּרֶךְ) "The Way": A Hebrew word meaning path, journey, or manner of walking. In this work, HaDerekh refers to a lived, embodied way of following God, not only through belief, but through breath, posture, movement, and daily life.

Tenuat HaDerekh (תנועת הדרך) "Movement of The Way": A sacred, breath-led movement practice rooted in the Hebrew letters as living forms. Tenuat HaDerekh invites the body into prayer, remembrance, and alignment through gentle, intentional movement.

Living Letters: The Hebrew Aleph-Bet understood not merely as written symbols, but as energetic, embodied forms. Each letter carries meaning, movement, sound, and spiritual invitation that can be experienced through the body.

Living Word: A term describing the Word of God as active, present, and embodied, rather than static or abstract. In Scripture, the Living Word refers both to the written Word (the Scriptures) and to the Word made flesh — Yeshua — who lived, taught, healed, and revealed God through embodied love and action. Within HaDerekh, "Living Word" also names the way divine truth is encountered through breath, movement, posture, and lived practice. The Word is not only read or spoken, but walked, breathed, and enacted through the body. The Living Word meets each person where they are, inviting relationship rather than performance, and transformation rather than mere belief.

Embodied Prayer: Prayer expressed through the body — through breath, posture, gesture, stillness, and movement. In embodied prayer, the whole person participates, not only the mind or voice.

Breath-Led Practice: A way of moving that follows the rhythm of natural breathing rather than force, effort, or external pacing. Breath guides timing, depth, and transition.

Adaptive Posture: A movement or position that can be practiced standing, seated, supported, or visualized. Adaptation honors different bodies, abilities, and seasons of life.

Consent (in Practice): An inner permission given by the practitioner to engage, pause, modify, or rest. Consent is foundational — nothing in this practice is forced.

Stillness: An intentional pause that allows awareness, listening, and presence. Stillness is considered an active form of practice, not an absence of movement.

Kli (כְּלִי) "Vessel": A Hebrew word meaning container, instrument, or vessel. In this work, the body is understood as a sacred kli, a vessel designed to carry, receive, and express the presence of God.

Nefesh (נֶפֶשׁ): Often translated as life-force or living being. Nefesh relates to the instinctual, physical, and grounding aspects of life, safety, rest, and embodied presence.

Neshamah (נְשָׁמָה): is associated with the breath of understanding or awareness, reflection, discernment, and conscious breathing.

Ruach (רוּחַ) Spirit: wind, or breath in motion. Ruach refers to creative flow, inspiration, and the animating Spirit of God expressed through movement and life.

Alignment: A state in which body, breath, intention, and spirit move together in harmony. Alignment is not perfection, but coherence and honesty.

Sacred Flow: A continuous sequence of movements guided by breath and intention, often moving through the Hebrew letters from Aleph to Tav. Sacred Flow emphasizes continuity, presence, and integration.

Aleph-Tav: The first and last letters of the Hebrew alphabet, symbolizing beginning to completion. Moving Aleph-Tav reflects wholeness, journey, and fulfillment.

Temple Imagery: Biblical imagery of the Temple used as a metaphor for the human body, heart, breath, spine, feet, and movement reflecting sacred spaces and functions.

Embodied Parallel: A way of understanding spiritual concepts through the body for example, the spine as the Ark, breath as the veil, or feet as the outer court.

Integration: The process of carrying the practice beyond formal movement into daily life, walking, working, resting, serving, and loving with awareness.

Teacher/Facilitator: A steward of space rather than an authority. In HaDerekh, a teacher guides gently, honors consent, and models presence rather than control.

Letters of Fire: A term referring to advanced or initiatory engagement with the practice, where movement becomes deeply internal, devotional, and responsive to the Spirit.

Amen: A Hebrew word meaning firm, faithful, so be it. In this practice, Amen may be spoken, breathed, or embodied as a closing of prayer and intention.

Logos (Λόγος): The Living Word: In the Scriptures, Logos refers to The Word through which God creates, reveals, and sustains life. In the Hebrew imagination, God's Word is never static, it acts, speaks, moves, and brings forth life. For Messianic believers, this Living Word is revealed fully in Yeshua (Jesus), who is described as The Word made flesh, God's truth embodied and walking among us. In this practice, Logos is encountered not only through reading or hearing, but through breath, posture, movement, and lived obedience. The Word is not only received; it is inhabited.

Shabbot: A sacred rhythm of rest, cessation, and delight. Shabbat is not merely the absence of work, but the intentional return to presence, trust, and communion with God. In embodied practice, Shabbat is expressed through slowing, breathing, stillness, and receiving rather than striving.

Eden: Often translated as "delight," Eden represents the original state of harmony between God, humanity, and creation. In this work, Eden symbolizes remembered wholeness, a return to right relationship through breath, movement, and embodied trust.

Sefirot (סְפִירוֹת): A term from Jewish mystical tradition referring to the divine attributes or emanations through which God's presence and character are revealed in the world. In this work, the Sefirot are understood not as energies to be controlled, but as sacred qualities such as wisdom, compassion, strength, and harmony that are embodied through faithful walking, prayer, breath, and movement aligned with God.

Otiyot: The Hebrew word for "letters." In Hebraic understanding, the Otiyot are more than written symbols; they are vessels of meaning through which God's Word creates, communicates, and sustains life. In HaDerekh, the Hebrew letters are engaged as Living Letters, embodied through posture, breath, sound, and attentive presence.

Living Letters

The Way of the Living Letters

In the Hebrew tradition, letters are not merely symbols on a page, they are living forms. Each letter carries breath, sound, movement, and meaning. Before words were written, they were spoken. Before they were spoken, they were breathed. And before they were breathed, they were held in the body.

The Living Letters invite us to remember that language itself was born from breath and motion. The Aleph begins as silent breath. The Bet opens into dwelling. The letters progress not only as an alphabet, but as a journey, from beginning to completion, from seed to fulfillment, from intention to embodiment.

Tenuat HaDerekh approaches the Hebrew letters not as concepts to be studied alone, but as invitations to be lived. Each letter becomes a posture, a breath, a stance of the body and heart. Through gentle movement and stillness, the practitioner learns to walk the letters, allowing Scripture to take shape not only in the mind, but in muscle, bone, breath, and nervous system. This is not performance, It is remembrance.

The Living Letters meet each person where they are. Movements may be strong or subtle, standing or seated, external or internal. What matters is not precision, but presence. The body already knows how to pray, and when given permission, it remembers. As you move through this book, you are not being asked to master a form, but to enter a relationship: with breath, with Scripture, with your own embodied faith.

This is the way of the Living Letters where belief becomes practice, practice becomes posture, and posture becomes prayer.

Begin slowly.
Begin gently.
Begin where you are.

What is Tenuat HaDerekh?

Tenuat HaDerekh means "Movement of The Way" in Hebrew. It is a sacred embodiment practice that integrates faith, breath, Hebrew letters, resonance, and postural flow rooted in Scripture and illuminated by the Living Word, God's revealed Word, understood both as Scripture and, for Messianic believers, as Yeshua (Jesus), the Word made flesh.

A Healing Practice for Body, Soul, and Spirit

This practice was birthed from a deep need for grounding, peace, and alignment, especially for those whose spirits live in the upper realms but whose bodies long to feel safe, connected, and whole. In a world of disembodiment, trauma, and noise, _Tenuat HaDerekh_ calls us back to the quiet path, the ancient way, where movement becomes prayer and breath becomes restoration.

Rooted in Scripture, Aligned by Spirit

The foundation of this practice is Yeshua's declaration in John 14:6:
Ani HaDerekh, ve-ha-Emet, ve-ha-Chayim
I am the Way, the Truth, and the Life.

Every movement in this system is built upon this walk of faith, _a halakha_ (way of walking) that embodies worship, healing, and alignment with God's presence.

This practice is not designed to strengthen the body for its own sake, nor to be observed or evaluated by others. It is an act of embodied prayer, a way of offering breath, posture, and presence to God. In the Hebraic understanding of worship, faith is lived, not merely spoken. When the body moves with intention, reverence, and attention toward God, prayer becomes visible.

What Makes This Practice Unique?

- **Hebrew Letter Poses:** movement based on the Aleph-Bet, each carrying ancient energetic and spiritual meaning
- **Breath + Resonance Integration:** using voice, frequency, sound, and silence to restore coherence
- **Chakra + Ray Mapping:** blending Hebrew mysticism with commonly known body energy systems for healing and understanding
- **Scripture & Affirmation Pairings:** every posture and sequence is rooted in The Word
- **Messianic Foundation:** a practice for believers walking the path of Yeshua, honoring Jewish roots

For Whom? Tenuat HaDerekh is for:

- Those seeking grounding after trauma or spiritual fatigue
- Dancers, worshipers, teachers, families and individuals
- Healers and caregivers needing restoration
- Anyone ready to walk in wholeness and holiness

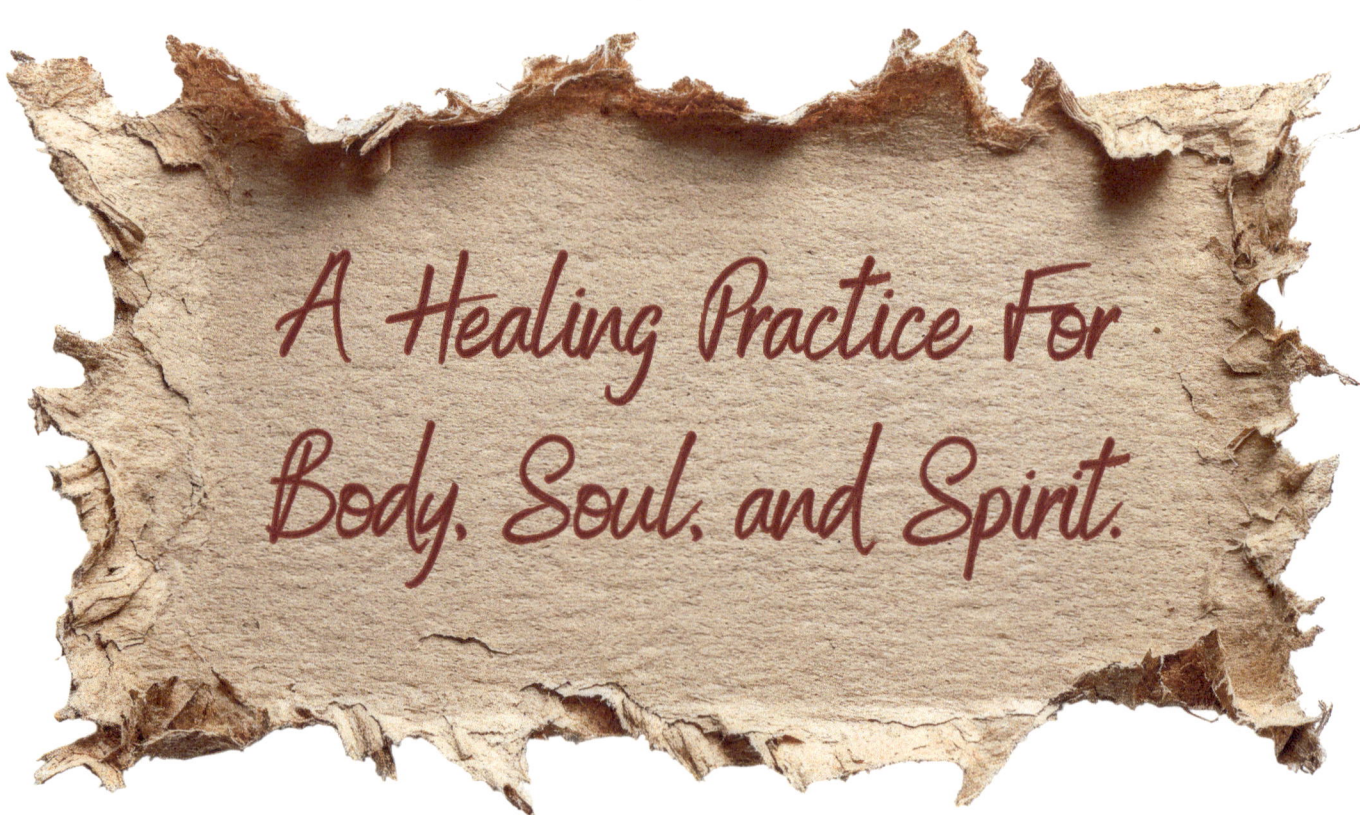

A Healing Practice For Body, Soul, and Spirit.

Foundation & Worship

Foundations & Worship

Before learning the movements themselves, we begin by understanding the spiritual and theological foundations that shape this practice.

1. Messianic Foundations

Rooted in the Way, the Truth, and the Life, Yeshua HaMashiach (Jesus the Messiah) this movement system honors the footsteps of the Messiah and the Spirit-breathed <u>halakha</u> (way of walking) He modeled.
"Whoever claims to live in Him must walk as Yeshua walked." 1 John 2:6
In Tenuat HaDerekh, the body is not a hindrance to the Spirit, it becomes the vessel of surrender, healing, and worship. The body is not an obstacle to worship, but a vessel through which prayer, obedience, and praise are expressed. The practice is Messianic in identity: grounded in Torah, fulfilled in Yeshua, and led by the Ruach (Spirit).

2. Hebraic Understanding of Body + Spirit

Ancient Hebrew thought views the body as whole, a vessel of the soul, a temple for the Spirit. Movement is not disconnected from prayer or worship. It is prayer in action.

- Words like <u>halakha</u> (הֲלָכָה) literally mean "the walk" or the path one lives out.
- The Hebrew word <u>derekh</u> (דֶּרֶךְ) means way but also lifestyle, manner, and journey.

This system honors the sacred rhythms of Sabbath, blessing, offering, repentance, and rejoicing, embodied in breath, gesture, and stillness.

3. Mystical Influence

From the Jewish mystical tradition, Tenuat HaDerekh draws gently on the energetic map of the <u>Sefirot</u>, the Tree of Life, and the vibrational power of the Hebrew letters, <u>Otiyot</u>.

- Each Hebrew letter becomes a living frequency, a posture, a sound
- Each Sefirah represents a divine attribute we embody in motion
- Each breath becomes a way to walk the inner and outer temple

This influence is not esoteric for its own sake, but serves the goal of alignment with The Divine, that we may walk in clarity, compassion, and coherence.

4. Embodied Worship

Finally, Tenuat HaDerekh is a love offering of movement as worship. Drawing from:

- Biblical dancers like Miriam and David
- Ancient temple postures of bowing, standing, lifting hands
- Contemporary needs for nervous system healing, trauma release, and somatic prayer

Tenuat HaDerekh recognizes that the body remembers and so we teach it again to remember whose we are. Everything in this practice flows from a single declaration.

Present your bodies as a living sacrifice holy and pleasing to God, this is your spiritual act of worship. Romans 12:1

Worship in Motion

- **Worship with the Whole Body**

Psalm 149:3 "Let them praise His name with dancing, making melody to Him with tambourine and lyre."
Embodied sense: Joy expressed through movement; praise that cannot stay still.

- **Unashamed Physical Praise**

2 Samuel 6:14 "David danced before the LORD with all his might, and David was wearing a linen ephod."
Embodied sense: Abandon, humility, and wholehearted devotion before God.

- **Posture of Reverence**

Psalm 95:6 "Oh come, let us worship and bow down; let us kneel before the LORD, our Maker."
Embodied sense: Kneeling, bowing, grounding the body in reverence.

- **Lifting the Body Toward God**

So I will bless You as long as I live; in Your name I will lift up my hands."
Embodied sense: Arms lifted, chest open, breath rising.

- **Stillness as Worship**

Psalm 131:2 "But I have calmed and quieted my soul, like a weaned child with its mother."
Embodied sense: Settling the nervous system; rest as devotion.

- **Worship That Involves the Breath**

Psalm 150:6 "Let everything that has breath praise the LORD."
Embodied sense: Breath itself becomes prayer, inhale and exhale as praise.

- **Walking the Way with God**

Psalm 119:1 "Blessed are those whose way is blameless, who walk in the Torah of the LORD."
Embodied sense: Faith lived through steps, rhythm, daily movement.

- **Miriam: Dance as Deliverance**

Exodus 15:20 "Miriam the prophetess... took a tambourine in her hand, and all the women went out after her with tambourines and dancing."
Embodied sense: Communal movement; celebration after deliverance.

- **Priestly Movement**

1 Chronicles 23:30 "They were to stand every morning, thanking and praising the LORD, and likewise at evening."
Embodied sense: Standing as ritual devotion; rhythm and repetition.

- **Worship Engaging the Senses**

Psalm 134:2 "Lift up your hands to the holy place and bless the LORD."
Embodied sense: Directional movement toward sacred space.

Miriam and David did not worship only with words, but with their whole bodies: feet that danced, knees that bowed, hands that lifted, and breath offered freely before God. The Movement of the Way continues this embodied worship, inviting us to praise not only with belief, but with movement.

Summary: A Holy Fusion

Tenuat HaDerekh is a fusion of:
- Messianic obedience
- Hebraic embodiment
- Mystical symbolism
- Holy Spirit movement

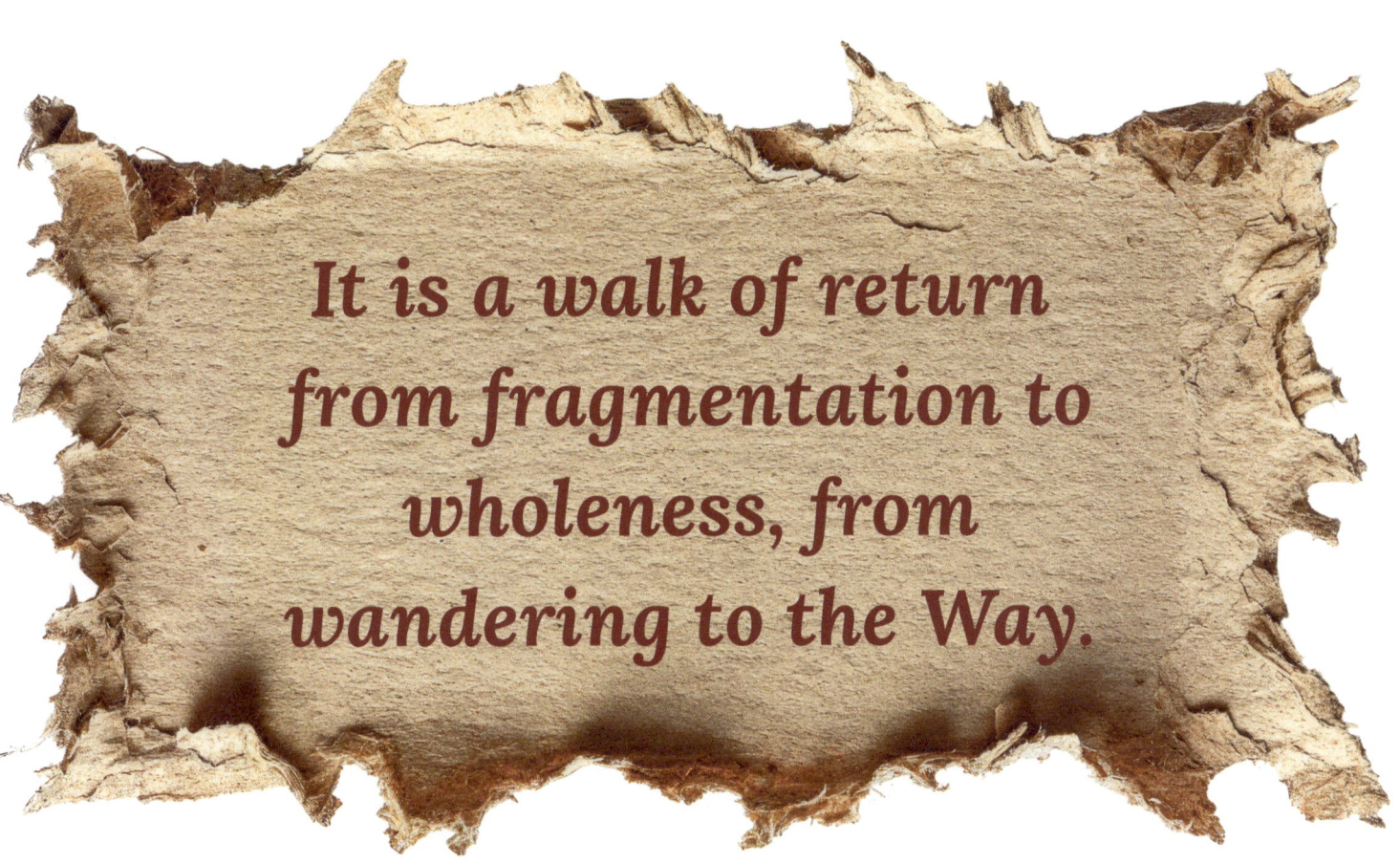

It is a walk of return from fragmentation to wholeness, from wandering to the Way.

Spiritual Interpretation

When Yeshua says <u>Ani ha-Derekh</u>, He is declaring:
- He is The Path we walk, not just a Teacher of Truth, but The Truth embodied.
- He is the journey and the destination.
- He is the new and ancient way back to the Father's heart.

Tenuat HaDerekh Application:

This verse is not just a foundation; it is the heartbeat of the practice. Each movement invites us to:
- Walk in The Way <u>HaDerekh</u>: posture, breath, surrender
- Stand in Truth <u>HaEmet</u>: aligned, stable, whole
- Live in Life <u>HaChayim</u>: joyfully, in Spirit and truth

Mantra Breath Practice:

Inhale: <u>Ani ha-Derekh</u>
Exhale: <u>Ve-ha-Emet, ve-ha-Chayim</u>

    Let this breath become a rhythm, a walking prayer.
    Let The Word become flesh in your body again.

Movement as Prayer

Faith is not static; it breathes. In Tenuat HaDerekh, movement is more than exercise. Movement of The Way is a sacred return, a way to reinhabit the body with intention, Scripture, and breath.

Before there was written prayer, there was gesture.
Before there were words, there was breath.
Before there was form, there was Spirit
hovering over the deep moving.

Movement Matters
- The Hebrew word <u>halakha</u> הֲלָכָה often translated "Jewish law" literally means "the walk."
- Faith is a path walked, not a rule recited.
- The prophets danced, lay prostrate, tore their garments, and lifted their hands.
- Worship was never confined to the lips, worship was embodied.
- Yeshua Himself walked miles, washed feet, wept, breathed on His disciples, and touched the sick.
- His ministry embodied movement.

In This Practice:
- We bow in surrender.
- We rise in praise.
- We breathe with the Spirit.
- We stretch in expectation.
- We flow like water.
- We still like the Shabbat.

Every movement is a prayer without words.
A return to Eden, a walk with the Father in the cool of the day.

Breath Mantra:
Inhale: This is my body...
Exhale: ...a living sacrifice. (Romans 12:1)

The Breath

RUACH, NESHAMA AND NEFESH

רוח

RUACH
SPIRIT / WIND
CREATIVE BREATH

FOCUS: Flow, cretivity, divine action

NESHAMA
BREATH OF GOD / HIGHER SOUL

FOCUS. Reflection, breath, clarity

MOVEMENT THEMES

NEFESH
VITAL SOUL / LIVING BEING

Grounding, safety
ROOT, REST, RELEASE

Ruach, Neshama, and Nefesh
Breath as the Divine Interface

In Hebraic understanding, we are not just "bodies with souls." We are multi-layered beings, animated by the Breath of God. The Hebrew Scriptures give us three primary words to describe this breath/soul/life interplay:

1. רוּחַ – <u>Ruach</u>
Spirit / Wind / Creative Breath
- Root meaning: Wind, invisible motion, power
- Function: The animating Spirit of God thru prophecy, power, renewal
- Location: The entire being, but often felt in the chest or spine
- Movement focus: Flow, inspired gestures, prophetic dance, spiral motion

> *In the beginning God created the heaven and the earth. And the earth was without form, and void; and darkness was upon the face of the deep. And the Spirit of God moved upon the face of the waters. Genesis 1:1-2*

> *Not by might, nor by power, but by My Spirit (Ruach), says the Lord. Zechariah 4:6*

2. נֶפֶשׁ – <u>Nefesh</u>
The Vital Soul / The Living Being / Life Force
- Root meaning: To breathe or exhale
- Function: Our instinctual life including hunger, safety, emotion, connection to the earth
- Location: Often associated with the blood or belly
- Movement focus: Grounding, resting, anchoring into the present moment

> *Let everything that has breath (<u>nefesh</u>) praise the Lord. Psalm 150:6*

3. נְשָׁמָה – <u>Neshama</u>

The Breath of God / Higher Soul
- Root meaning: To breathe gently
- Function: Our consciousness, reason, conscience, and spiritual reflection
- Location: Often associated with the head or face
- Movement focus: Clarity, stillness, breath awareness, upward stretch

And He breathed into his nostrils the breath, <u>neshama</u>, of life. Genesis 2:7

Summary: The Breath Body

Level of Being	Hebrew Word	Core Focus	Movement Themes
Instinct / Body	Nefesh (נֶפֶשׁ)	Safety, grounding, life-force	Rooting, rest, release, gentle containment
Thought / Soul	Neshamah (נְשָׁמָה)	Reflection, awareness, understanding	Breath awareness, clarity, stillness, lift
Spirit	Ruach (רוּחַ)	Flow, creativity, divine movement	Spiral motion, reach, inspired gesture, dance

In practice, these levels rise and fall together, guided always by breath.

Embodied Hebrew Understanding:
The Body as Vessel and Sanctuary
The body in Hebrew thought is not disposable or shameful, the body is a dwelling place (*mishkan*) and a sacrifice offered in love.
- Hands bless
- Feet carry good news
- Heart thinks and feels
- Bones rejoice (Psalm 35:10)
- The back bears the Name of God (as seen in the priestly garments)

When you move, you proclaim truth, not just in voice, but in muscle and breath.

Present your bodies as a living sacrifice... Romans 12:1

The Body

The Body as a Vessel of Light

In Hebraic thought, the body is not something to transcend or reject, the body is a vessel, a dwelling place, a living tabernacle through which the Spirit expresses itself.

And The Word became flesh and dwelt among us... John 1:14

The Hebrew word שָׁכֵן (*shakhan*) means to dwell, and is the root of Shekhinah, the indwelling Presence of God

This means the human body is capable of housing divine presence. Not only in stillness, but in movement. Movement becomes prayer when it is offered with intention, reverence, and attention toward God.

The Body in the Hebrew Bible:
- Hands are used to bless, lay on, or lift in praise
- Feet carry the Good News (Isaiah 52:7)
- The spine is the "ladder" Jacob saw a bridge between heaven and earth
- Bones rejoice (Psalm 35:10), tremble (Habakkuk 3:16), or prophesy (Ezekiel 37)
- The face shines with divine light (Moses' glowing face in Exodus 34)

My heart and my flesh cry out for the living God. Psalm 84:2

כְּלִי The Body as a Kli

A Sacred Vessel. In Hebrew, the word kli means vessel, container, or instrument

*We have this treasure in earthen vessels (klei cheres),
to show that the surpassing power belongs to
God and not to us. 2 Corinthians 4:7*

The body is not separate from the spiritual journey, it is the site of transformation. Every gesture, every breath, every posture is part of how we carry, receive, and pour out the divine.

Temple Imagery in the Body: When you move with intention, you re-enact temple service, you become the offering, the altar, the priest, and the flame. (See graph on opposite page.)

*You were bought with a price
therefore glorify God in your body.
1 Corinthians 6:20*

Summary:
The body is not a burden, it is the canvas of worship. Movement awakens memory, heals trauma, restores alignment. Every breath is a prayer, every step a pilgrimage, every movement a yes.

Temple Element	Temple Function	Embodied Parallel	Movement / Practice Expression
Holy of Holies	Dwelling place of God's Presence	Heart / Breath Center	Stillness, inward listening, reverent pause
Ark of the Covenant	Carrier of Torah, memory, covenant	Spine / Core axis	Upright posture, spinal awareness, sacred alignment
Altar	Place of offering and transformation	Solar Plexus / Will	Bowing, lifting, offering gestures
Veil	Boundary between seen and unseen	Breath / Threshold	Inhale-exhale transitions, crossing movements
Outer Court	Place of approach and preparation	Feet / Walking body	Grounding steps, intentional walking
Lampstand (Menorah)	Light, illumination	Eyes / Awareness	Gaze softening, orientation to light
Table of Bread	Sustenance, provision	Hands / Receiving	Open palms, receiving gestures
Priestly Service	Daily devotion and care	Whole body in motion	Flowing sequences, embodied prayer

**The temple was never meant to be left behind.
It was meant to be walked, breathed, and inhabited.**

The Role of Movement in Scripture

From Genesis to Revelation, movement is revelation. In the Hebrew worldview, movement is not separate from worship it is a sacred expression of intention, emotion, covenant, and Spirit. The body was never excluded from divine encounters. It was where they happened.

David: Dancing with Abandon

> And David danced before the LORD with all his might...
> 2 Samuel 6:14

- David's body became a vessel of joyful worship.
- His dance carried the Ark of the Covenant, the Presence of God back to Jerusalem.
- His movement was prophetic, royal, and vulnerable.

Tenuat Application:
Dance becomes an act of return, joy, and surrender.
We move to restore what belongs in the holy place.

Miriam: Leading with Tambourine and Dance

> Then Miriam the prophetess... took a tambourine
> in her hand, and all the women followed her,
> with tambourines and dancing. Exodus 15:20

- The first act of praise after Israel crossed the Red Sea was embodied movement.
- Miriam led the women in rhythmic celebration, marking liberation through step and song.

Tenuat Application:
We use movement to remember miracles.
Dance becomes remembrance and testimony.

Ezekiel: Prophetic Posture

> Lie on your left side... Ezekiel 4:4
> I fell on my face... — Ezekiel 1:28

- Ezekiel's body became symbol and sermon.
- He was told to act out visions, to embody prophecy.
- His physical stillness, laying down, and bowing were not passive. They were active obedience.

Tenuat Application:

Sometimes posture is the prophecy.
Stillness can speak louder than speech.

The Priests: Movement in the Temple

- Every priestly task required movement:
  - Washing
  - Carrying fire
  - Waving offerings
  - Stepping into the Holy of Holies
- Even garments were designed for fluidity of motion and sound.

Tenuat Application:

Movement becomes ministry.
Your body becomes a portable temple, moving in rhythm with heaven.

Yeshua: Touching, Walking, Weeping

"He stretched out His hand"

"He walked among them"

"He wept"

Yeshua's ministry was entirely embodied.

- He healed with touch.
- He taught as He walked.
- He kneeled to wash.
- He breathed on His disciples.
- He became flesh and moved among us.

Tenuat Application:

We follow The Way not just with belief but with movement.

Each gesture becomes an echo of His love.

Summary

Figure	Embodied Action	Movement Expression	Spiritual Function
David	Dance before the Lord	Joyful, unrestrained movement	Return of the heart; wholehearted worship
Miriam	Tambourine & dance	Rhythmic movement, communal expression	Celebration, prophetic leadership
Ezekiel	Prostration / posture	Falling, rising, attentive stillness	Prophetic obedience; surrender
Priests	Ritual movement	Repeated gestures, ordered flow	Service, intercession, continuity
Yeshua	Touch, walking, gesture	Healing touch, shared movement, embodied presence	Healing, compassion, love made flesh

The Way of God has always been known through the body through waking, bowing, dancing, touching, and weeping.

How to Use This Book

A Guide for Readers, Practitioners, and Teachers

This book is not meant to be rushed.

HaDerekh, The Way is a movement-based, breath-led practice rooted in the Hebrew letters as living forms. Each letter offers an invitation into embodied prayer, reflection, and alignment, not as a performance, but as a manner of being. The movements that follow are not performed for mastery, but received as invitations into prayerful presence.

You may engage this book in several ways.

For Personal Practice

You may move through the letters slowly, one at a time, allowing each posture, breath, and reflection to settle into your body. Some readers will choose to practice a single letter for days or weeks. Others follow the sequence intuitively. There is no required pace.

Silence is welcome. Stillness is practice.

For Group or Class Settings

Trained teachers and facilitators may guide individuals or groups through selected letters or through the full Aleph–Tav Sacred Flow. The practice is adaptable for standing, seated, or mixed ability participants. Movements may be modified, visualized, or expressed through breath alone.

Participants are always encouraged to honor their own bodies and boundaries.

For Teaching & Facilitation

This book is designed to support instructors, chaplains, clergy, movement teachers, and caregivers. The written cues may be read aloud, paraphrased, or held internally. Optional tools such as voice, silence, or simple sound instruments may be used, but are not required.

The primary guide is presence.

On Breath, Movement, and Meaning

Breath instructions are offered as gentle suggestions. Postures are symbolic, not prescriptive. Reflection phrases may be spoken, whispered, or held silently. Scripture is included as grounding, not as obligation. If at any point a movement does not feel supportive, you may pause, rest, or return to breath.

On Endings

Multiple closing blessings are included near the end of this book. Teachers and readers may choose the closing that best serves their setting or choose silence. Completion is not marked by finishing the book, but by integration into daily life.

A Final Word

This book is a companion, not a destination. You are invited to return to it as you would return to a path again and again, with curiosity, with reverence, and with trust.

Some letters may appear more than once throughout the book, serving as anchors for beginning, integration, or rest.

Gentle Guide for Walking the Way

Tenuat HaDerekh — Movement of The Way — is not a program to complete, but a path to walk. This book is designed to meet you where you are and invite you into embodied prayer, breath, and Scripture at a pace that honors both body and spirit.

There is no single "right way" to move through these pages. Allow the practice to unfold slowly, as a companion you may return to again and again.

Begin with presence, not perfection. You do not need flexibility, prior movement experience, or theological expertise to begin. You only need willingness. Move gently. Breathe naturally. Pause often. If at any point you feel overwhelmed, distracted, or tired, rest. Rest is part of the practice.

Choose what is life-giving.

Each Hebrew letter posture includes movement, breath, Scripture, and reflection. You may engage with one element or all of them. Some days, the posture may be too much, and the breath alone is enough. This is still prayer.

Honor your body. Your body is not an obstacle to holiness — it is a vessel of worship. All movements may be practiced seated, supported, or adapted. You may stop, modify, or rest at any time. Pain is never a requirement for spiritual growth.

Let Scripture lead.

Scripture is the foundation of this practice. Movement does not replace prayer, it becomes prayer. Allow the Word to settle not only in your thoughts, but in your breath, posture, and stillness.

Go slowly.

You may practice one letter a day, repeat a single posture for a week, or return to familiar movements during seasons of fatigue or transition. There is no finish line. Faithfulness is the practice. Tenuat HaDerekh is an invitation to remember: that your body belongs in prayer, that breath is sacred, and that the Way is walked, not rushed.

The Hebrew Letter Movement Poses are based on the Aleph-Bet and form the embodied foundation of this practice.

"What am I looking at?"

Tenuat HaDerekh is an invitation to remember that your body belongs in prayer, that breath is sacred, and that the Way is not hurried but walked — step by step, in presence and trust.

Each posture includes posture shape, breath, Scripture, and reflection.

If you feel unsure, return to breath.
Breath is always the beginning and the place of return.

If the posture is not accessible, remain with the breath and intention.

Your body belongs in prayer.

There is nothing to memorize.
You may read, listen, move, or simply rest with the page.
The practice meets you where you are.

Optional tools may be used to round out your prayer time.
These may include simple sounds, frequency, chromotherapy, timing supports, or other gentle aids that help mark transitions or sustain attention. Tools do not lead the practice — presence does.

Some letters may appear more than once throughout the book, serving as anchors for beginning, integration, or rest.

Optional Tools for Teachers & Facilitators

Tenuat HaDerekh is a breath-led, body-based practice. No external tools are required.

Some teachers may choose to incorporate simple sound or timing tools to support pacing, transitions, or atmosphere. These are offered as optional supports, not necessities.

Primary Tool:
Breath, voice, silence, and embodied presence

Optional Supports:
- Tuning forks (used gently, often off-body)
- Singing bowls, bells, or chimes
- Chromotherapy & Colored Light
- Soft percussion for timing or transitions

Tools are not meant to lead the practice, but to serve it.

When in doubt, return to breath, stillness, and the body.

MOVEMENT AS PRAYER

האמנוה הושמת

Faith is not static; it breathes.

Hebrew Letter Movements (Aleph-Tav)

א ALEPH — *The Silent Breath*

Activation Phrase

I begin in stillness.
I am held in the breath of the One.
I carry no sound only presence.

Breath

Breath of Beginning
Inhale gently through the nose for a count of 4
Hold the breath in stillness for 4
Exhale softly through the mouth or nose for 6
Repeat 3–7 times.
Let stillness expand. Eyes may close or gaze slightly upward.

Scripture

Be still and know that I am God. Psalm 46:10
The Breath of the Almighty gives me life. Job 33:4

963 ♫B

- Awareness & Rest
- White

ב BET — House, Dwelling, Container

Activation Phrase

I am a dwelling place of peace. The Holy One abides in me.

Breath

"Breath of Belonging"
- Inhale gently through the nose, feeling the breath fill your "inner house" (4 count)
- Pause and rest in that fullness (hold 3)
- Exhale slowly, imagining the light from within extending outward (6 count)

Repeat 3–5 times, dwelling in warmth and inner blessing.

Scripture

Blessed are those who dwell in Your house. Psalm 84:4

Do you not know that you are God's temple and that God's Spirit dwells in you? 1 Corinthians 3:16

528 ♪♫E
- Heart
- Green/Yellow

ב

ג GIMEL   *The Giving Flow*

Activation Phrase

I step forward in love. I carry light into barren places.

My giving is guided by grace.

Breath

Inhale: Expand heart and feel the weight shift slightly forward.

Exhale: Allow your body to soften into the pose, anchoring through your grounded foot.

Optional: Whisper "Gimel... Grace flows forward."

Scripture

Give, and it will be given to you. A good measure, pressed down, shaken together and running over... Luke 6:38

He has told you, O man, what is good... to do justice, love mercy, and walk humbly with your God. Micah 6:8

528

- *Heart*
- *Green*

ד DALET — The Door - Humble Acess

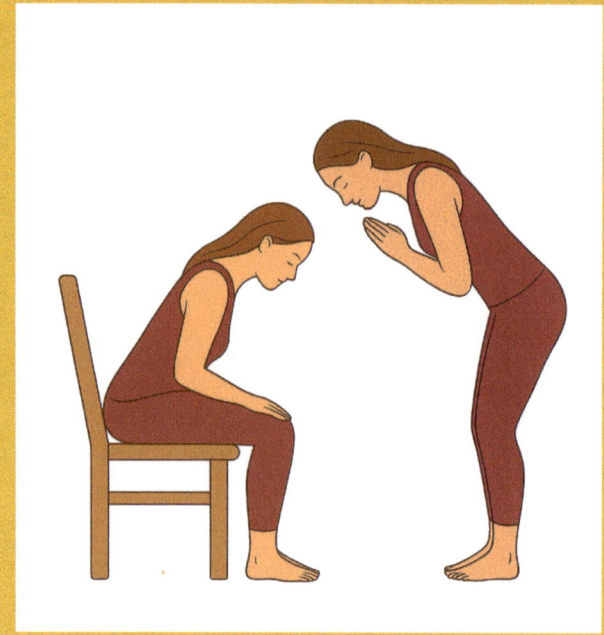

Activation Phrase

The humble will see their prayers answered. Yeshua, the Door, welcomes those who knock with faith.

Breath

Threshold Breath
- Inhale through the nose (count 5): expand the heart space.
- Pause briefly: "I am standing at the door."
- Exhale through soft pursed lips (count 7): release resistance and self-will.
- Repeat 3–7 times to enter a state of humble readiness.

Scripture

Behold, I stand at the door and knock... Revelation 3:20

I am the door. If anyone enters by Me, he will be saved, and will go in and out and find pasture. John 10:9

Open for me the gates of righteousness; I will enter and give thanks to the LORD. Psalm 118:19

Lift up your heads, O you gates; be lifted up, you ancient doors, that the King of glory may come in. Psalms 24:7

417 ♪♪D

- Strength
- Orange

T

 # HEY

Breath of Revelations

Activation Phrase
I open to receive the Breath of Life. Revelation lives in my inhale and exhale. Holy Spirit, breathe through me.

Breath

"The Descent of Light"
Posture: Stand or sit tall in the Hey – Breath Gate posture. Spine long, chest open, palms lifted or gently facing upward.

- Inhale (963 Hz – Note B): Breathe slowly through the crown visualizing radiant white-gold light entering from above.
- Whisper inwardly: "I receive the breath of life." Sense the top of your head tingling or expanding as awareness opens. Hold (2-3 count): Let that light hover — luminous, weightless — at the top of your being. Feel divine clarity and stillness.
- Exhale (528 Hz – Note C): Allow the breath to descend through the chest into the heart. Visualize emerald-green light spiraling downward, merging heaven's wisdom with human love.
- Whisper outwardly: "Love becomes life within me." Repeat 3-7 cycles — each time feeling more integration between crown and heart, heaven and earth.

Scripture

The Spirit of God has made me; the breath of the Almighty gives me life. Job 33:4

May the love of God be poured into our hearts by the Holy Spirit. Romans 5:5

963 ♪♪A → 528 ♪♪C

- Mind / Discernment
- Indigo
- Job 33:4

- Heart
- Green
- Ps 46:10

 **HEY**   *Revelation & Awakening*

Activation Phrase

Revelation lives in my inhale and exhale.
Holy Spirit, breathe through me.

Breath

"The Window of Revelation"
- Posture : Stand or sit tall (Breath-Gate or standing Hey pose). Lengtenhen the spine; soften the jaw and shoulders.
- Inhale (Count 4–5) — Draw the breath through the crown into the brow. Whisper inwardly: "Receive the breath of life."
- Hold (Count 2–3) — Sense a quiet light expanding behind the forehead, as if a window is opening.
- Exhale (Count 6–7) — Release gently through parted lips, allowing a soft audible "Hhhhey..." sound. Whisper outwardly: "Reveal Your truth through me."
- Repeat 3–7 cycles, keeping the breath luminous and unforced. Eyes may close or gaze upward toward the brow center.

Scripture

Then the LORD God breathed into his nostrils the breath of life. Genesis 2:7

The entrance of Your word gives light; it gives understanding to the simple. Psalm 119:130

852 ♪♫A

- *Mind / Discernment*
- *Violet*

ו VAV   The Bridge Between

Activation Phrase

I am a bridge.
Heaven and earth meet within me.
I stand in the center.
Whole, connected, and *aligned*.

Breath

The Connecting Line

Inhale gently up from the soles of your feet to the crown of your head (count 5) - Hold in stillness (count 2) - Exhale from crown to earth (count 5)

Visualize a vertical column of golden light flowing through your spine — Heaven and Earth in continuous exchange.

Scripture

Your kingdom come, Your will be done, on earth as it is in heaven. Matthew 6:10

And the Word became Flesh and dwelt among us… John 1:14

369 ♪♫ E

- *Strength*
- *Golden Yellow*

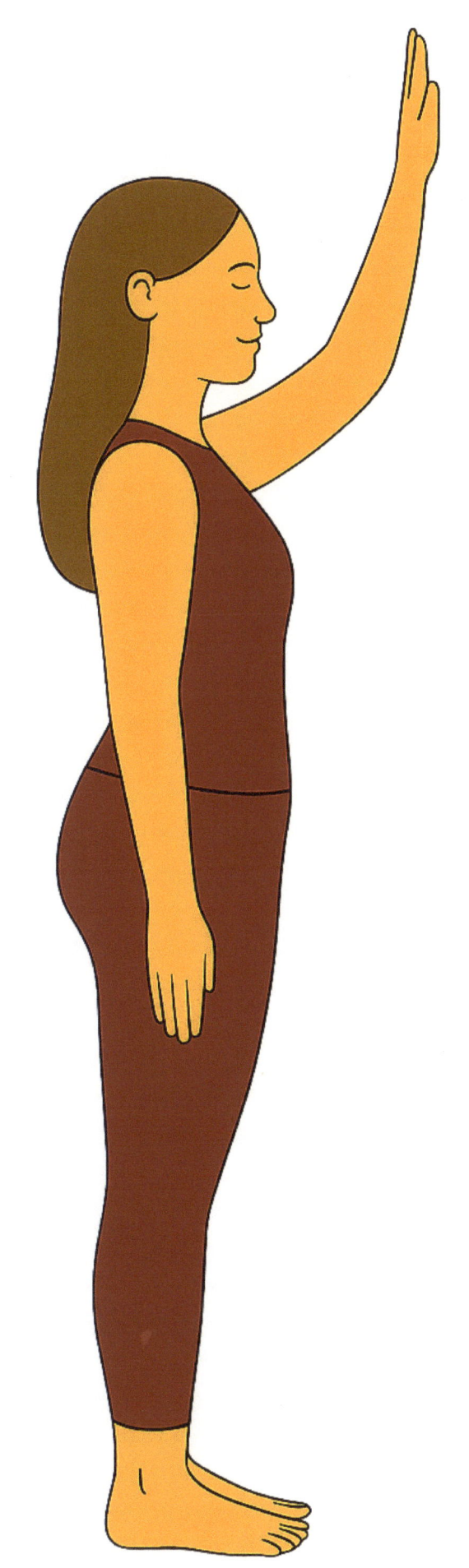

ז ZAYIN — Covenant Blade

Activation Phrase

*I wield truth with love.
I am sustained
by the Word.*

Breath

Inhale — Draw energy up from the earth into the heart.
Exhale — Extend light outward through the open hand.
Repeat 3 times while silently affirming:
"I carry peace as my shield, and truth as my sword."

Scripture

The Word of God is living and active, sharper than any two edged sword...
Hebrews 4:12
I am YHVH who heals you."
Exodus 15 : 26

693 ♫F

- Heart
- Violet

ז ZAYIN   *Crown Blade*

Activation Phrase

I speak what Heaven speaks.
Truth flows through me like light.
My mind is illumined by the Word.

Breath

Inhale — Draw energy up from the earth into the heart.
Exhale — Extend light outward through the open hand.
Repeat 3 times while silently affirming:
"I receive truth from above. I wield it with love."

Scripture

Take the helmet of salvation and the sword of the Spirit, which is the Word of God.
Ephesians 6 : 17

963 ♩♪B

- Awareness / Rest
- White

ח CHET — *The Inner Chamber*

Activation Phrase

I am a living sanctuary.
I welcome the Beloved within.
I dwell in the secret place of the Most High.
I abide beneath the Shadow of the Almighty.

Breath

"Breath of Covenant"
Inhale: Feel yourself stepping into the holy chamber of your soul. You dwell in safety.
Exhale: Release resistance and let your heart be seen. Life is guarded here. Repeat ×3 while softly whispering:
"I enter the chamber of my soul with truth and tenderness."

Scripture

He who dwells in the secret place of the Most High shall abide under the shadow of the Almighty. Psalm 91 : 1

285 🎵B

- *Heart*
- *Green*

ט TET — *Hidden Goodness*

Activation Phrase

Within me lies divine goodness waiting to unfold. I embrace the sacred space of becoming — the mystery within the hidden place. I am being formed by Love, from the inside out.

Breath

Inhale deeply through the nose — hold briefly in stillness.

Exhale slowly through the mouth, releasing tension while retaining inner warmth.

With each breath, imagine divine light forming within your core — unseen yet alive.

Scripture

For You formed my inward parts; You knit me together in my mother's womb. I praise You, for I am fearfully and wonderfully made. Psalm 139 : 13–14

God saw all that He had made, and it was good. Genesis 1:31

528 ♫B

- *Heart*
- *Rose - Pink*

YOD

The Divine Point

Activation Phrase

I am a spark of divine creation. Within me burns the light of the Eternal. I rise in love, balanced and whole.

Breath

Breath of Spark
- Inhale — draw light from the soles of your feet up through your spine.
- Hold — feel the spark ignite in your heart.
- Exhale — release through the crown, offering the light back to Source.
- Repeat slowly 3–5 times.

Scripture

Let your light so shine before others, that they may see your good works and glorify your Father in heaven. Matthew 5:16

You send forth Your Spirit, and they are created; You renew the face of the earth. Psalm 104:30

963 B

- *Awareness / Rest*
- *White Violet*

YOD — *The Spark*

Activation Phrase

I carry the spark of the Holy One.
I begin in Light.
Even in stillness,
I shine.

Breath

Inhale: Receive the breath of life.
Hold briefly: Feel the light expand within.
Exhale: Let the spark of love radiate outward.

Scripture

Before I formed you in the womb I knew you. Jeremiah 1 : 5
For I am YHVH your God who takes hold of your right hand and says to you, Do not fear; I will help you. Isaiah 41:13

963 ♪♫B

- Awareness / Rest
- White Violet

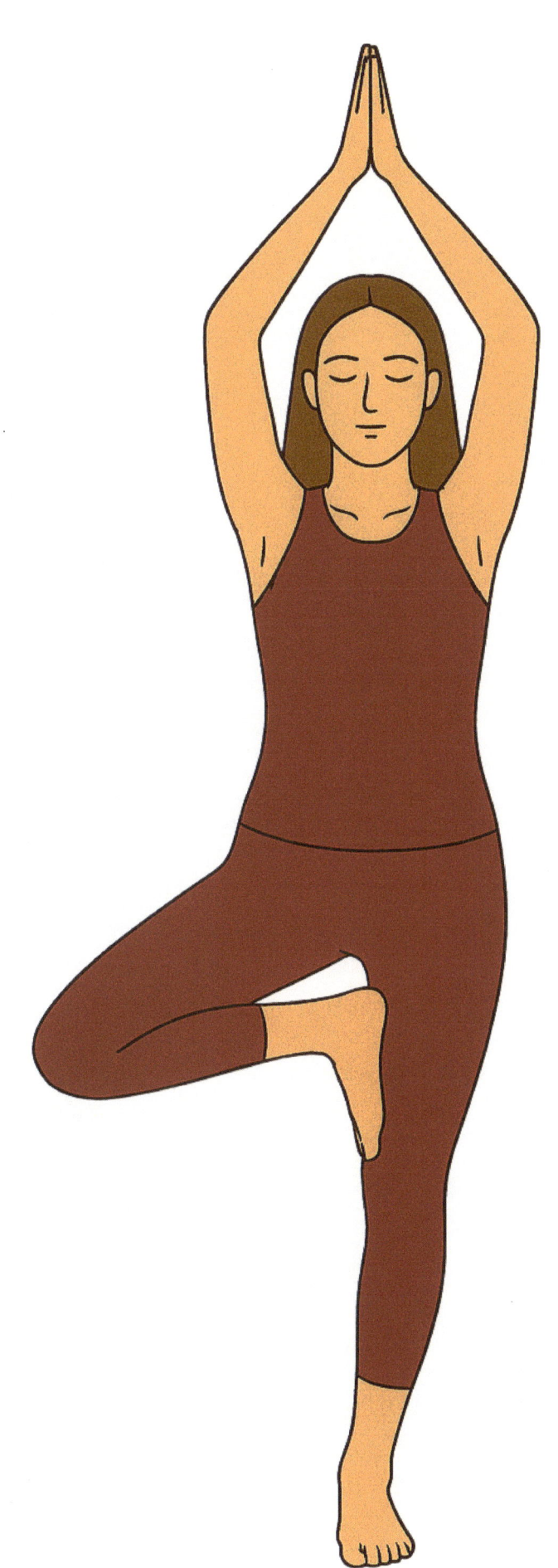

כ KAF — *The Blessed Vessel*

Activation Phrase
I open my hands and heart in surrender.
As I yield, I am filled.
As I release, I am blessed.
I am a vessel for peace a conduit of blessing.

Breath
Inhale — hold — exhale slowly through the mouth.
With each exhale, release control; with each inhale, receive peace.

Scripture
The Lord bless you and keep you; the Lord make His face shine upon you and be gracious to you; the Lord lift up His countenance upon you and give you peace. Numbers 6:24–26

432 🎵A
- *Heart*
- *Green*

ל LAMED   The Staff That Reaches

Activation Phrase

Illuminate my path and teach me Your ways.
I am taught as I rise.
*Let your raised hand become the staff of divine learning.
Let your heart become the flame that carries it forward.*

Breath

Inhale: Slowly raise your arms in a vertical arc, palms facing each other. Exhale: Root your feet, draw in divine light, and expand your chest in openness. Optional: Hold for a few breaths at the peak, eyes softly gazing upward or closed in reverence.

Scripture

Teach me, O YHVH, the way of Your statutes, and I shall keep it to the end. Psalm 119:33

741 ♫B

- Breath
- Violet

7

מ MEM — Womb of Waters

Activation Phrase
I dwell in the deep.
I am held in holy waters.
What is forming within me will rise in its time.

Breath
Inhale gently through the nose, allowing the belly to expand as though filling a sacred bowl with water.
Exhale slowly through the mouth, imagining soft ripples moving outward across a still pond.
Repeat 3–5 rounds. Let the body feel held, not pushed.

Scripture
Deep calls unto deep at the noise of Your waterfalls; all Your waves and billows have gone over me. Psalm 42:7

417 ♪♪D
- *Strength*
- *Blue*

נ NUN — The Humble Path

Activation Phrase

I bend so I may rise renewed.

Breath

Inhale gently — receiving grace.
Exhale slowly — bowing in gratitude.
Let each breath carry awareness of divine strength in your yielding.

Scripture

He leads the humble in what is right, and teaches the humble His way. Psalm 25 : 9

639 ♪♫F
- *Heart*
- *Green*

ס SAMEKH — The Circle of Support

Activation Phrase

I am encircled by Divine Light. I rest in the strength that upholds all things. The Everlasting Arms surround me.

Breath

Inhale slowly — feel yourself upheld.
Pause in stillness.
Exhale — release into divine trust.

Scripture

The eternal God is your refuge, and underneath are the everlasting arms. Deuteronomy 33 : 27

God is our refuge and strength, an ever-present help in trouble. Psalm 46:1

528 ♫F

- Heart
- Green

 AYIN — To See Beyond Seeing

Activation Phrase
I close my eyes to see more clearly.
Open the eyes of my heart, O Holy One.
Let me see as You see with love, wisdom, and grace.

Breath
Inhale — "I rest in trust."
Exhale — "I open to insight."
Repeat slowly 3–5 times, allowing the forehead and heart to soften.

Scripture
Open my eyes, that I may behold wondrous things out of Your Torah. Psalm 119 : 18

639 ♫F
- Heart
- Green

 **PEI** — *Sacred Speech & Living Breath*

Activation Phrase

My words create worlds.
I breathe blessing into being.
May every breath become praise.

Breath

Inhale through the nose, slowly:
"Receive the Ruach — the Breath of God."
Exhale gently through parted lips as the hand extends:
"I speak life. I release peace."
Repeat 3–5 times, allowing breath and intention to align.

Scripture

Let the words of my mouth and the meditation of my heart be acceptable in Your sight, O Lord, my Rock and my Redeemer." Psalm 19:14
"Your tongue has the power of life and death... Proverbs 18:21
So shall My word be that goes forth from My mouth; It shall not return to Me void, But it shall accomplish what I please, And it shall prosper in the thing for which I sent it. Isaiah 55:11

731 ♪♪G

- Breath
- Blue

 TZADEI — Righteous Surrender

Activation Phrase

May I walk upright in hidden faith.
Let righteousness root me, and mercy crown me.

Breath

With each exhale: release ego, pride, or self-assertion.
With each inhale: receive divine alignment and clarity.
Let the bow become a conversation — surrender met by guidance.

Scripture

The righteous will flourish like a palm tree; they will grow like a cedar of Lebanon. Psalm 92:12

396 ♪♪F

- *Grounding*
- *Deep Red*

17 QOF — Sanctified Threshold

Activation Phrase

I am set apart, not above.
I rise in holiness by
Your light alone.
or, for those in stillness:
Even here, I am found.
Even here,
I am made holy.

Breath

Inhale: "Sanctify me in Your truth."
Exhale: "Let my life rise to meet You."

Scripture

Sanctify them by the truth; Your word is truth. John 17:17

Who may ascend the mountain of the LORD? Who may stand in His holy place? One who has clean hands and a pure heart. Psalm 24:3-4

Light dawns in the darkness for the upright. Psalm 112:4 & 2 Corinthians 6:17

396 ♪♫G

- *Grounding*
- *Deep Red*

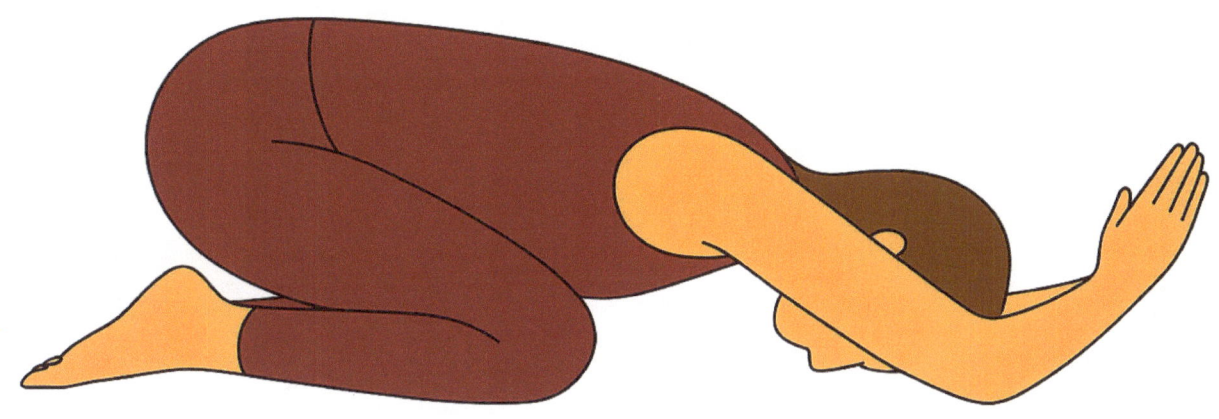

17

ר RESH — The Beginning of Return

Activation Phrase

I bow to the One who makes all things new.
In humility,
I find my highest posture.

Breath

Inhale: "You lift my head…"
Exhale: "And call me to rise anew."
Inhale: "You lift my head…"
Exhale: "And restore my glory."

Scripture

Return to Me, and I will return to you. Malachi 3:7

417 ♪♫F
- Heart
- Green

 SHIN

Flame of Revelation
Flame of Divine Presence

Activation Phrase
Kindle the flame within me,
O Holy One. Let me burn
with Your presence,
yet never be consumed.
Let the fire be
transformation not
destruction.
Let the light rise through me,
revealing what is holy.

Breath
Inhale as if drawing flame through the crown of your head

Exhale through your heart, warming the space around you

Let your breath rise like incense, uniting heaven and earth.

Scripture
Our God is a consuming fire.
Hebrews 12:29 & Deut. 4:24
The bush burned with fire but was not consumed.
Exodus 3:2

963 ♪♫B
- Awareness / Rest
- White

ש

ת TAV — *Mark of Completion*

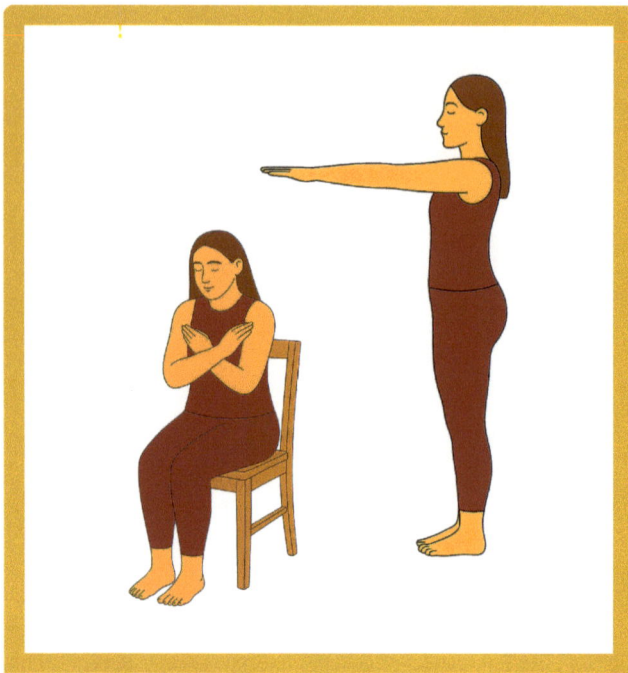

Activation Phrase
I open my hands and heart in surrender.
As I yield, I am filled.
As I release,
I am blessed.
I am a vessel for peace

Breath: Inhale: "I receive the seal of Your truth."
Exhale: "I rest in Your completeness."
Let each breath be an agreement — a quiet Yes to divine timing and eternal presence.

Scripture
I am the Aleph and the Tav, the Beginning and the End.
Revelation 22:13

396 ♫B
- Awareness / Rest
- White

ת

Sacred Flow Aleph-Tav Integration

SACRED FLOW PRACTICE

Tenuat HaDerekh
The Full Aleph–Tav Flow

Theme: Walking The Way from Breath → Body → Return → Completion

Total time: ~ 30 minutes approximately
Adaptable: standing, seated, or mixed-ability circle

OPENING: Stillness & Consent — 2 minutes

Aleph (א)

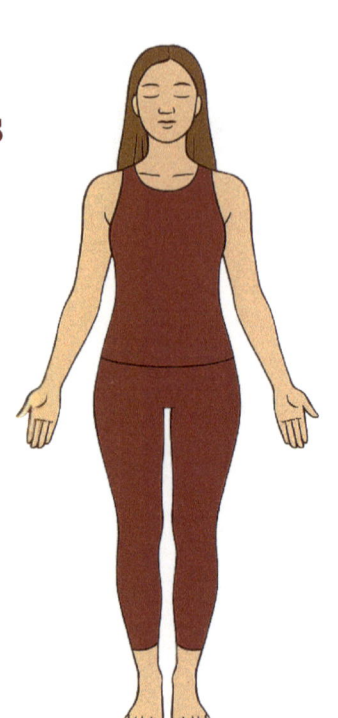

- Silent standing or seated stillness
- Breath of Beginning
- Mantra (soft or inward):
- "Ani ha-Derekh…"

SECTION 1: INDWELLING & OFFERING - HEART AWAKING

Bet → Gimel → Dalet

- Bet (ב) Inner dwelling
- Gimel (ג) Step forward in grace
- Dalet (ד) Bow / Threshold of humility

Flow cue:
"From dwelling → to giving → to asking."

SECTION 2: Revelation & Connection - Vertical Alignment

Hey → Vav → Zayin

- Hey (ה) Arms lift, breath descends
- Vav (ו) Vertical bridge, one hand heart / one hand heaven
- Zayin (ז) Sword of truth (gentle, not forceful

Flow cue:
"Receive → connect → discern."

SECTION 3: Sanctuary & Formation - Inner Healing

Chet → Tet → Yod

- Chet (ח) Enter the inner chamber
- Tet (ט) Curl inward, hidden goodness
- Yod (י) Small spark, seated or standing

Flow cue:
"Receive → connect → discern."

SECTION 4: Teaching & Waters - Expression & Mercy

Kaf → Lamed → Mem

- Kaf (כ) Open hands / receive blessing
- Lamed (ל) Reach upward in learning
- Mem (מ) Self-embrace / womb of waters

Flow cue:
"Receive → rise → soften."

SECTION 5: Support & Seeing - Trust & Perception

Nun → Samekh → Ayin

- Nun (נ) Bow / humility
- Samekh (ס) Encircling arms of support
- Ayin (ע) Hands to eyes / inner vision

Flow cue:
"Yield → trust → perceive."

SECTION 6: Speech & Righteousness - Embodied Truth

Pei → Tzadei → Qof

- Pei (פ) One hand mouth, one hand offering
- Tzadei (צ) Prostration / righteous surrender
- Qof (ק) Rising from the threshold

Flow cue:
"Speak → surrender → rise."

SECTION 7: Return & Fire - Completion

Resh → Shin → Tav

- Resh (ר) Bowed return
- Shin (ש) Flame of divine presence
- Tav (ת) Seal of completion (arms crossed or wide)

Closing Breath:
Inhale: "I receive Your seal."
Exhale: "Amen."

Closing & Integration

The Way Walked

You have walked The Way.
You have breathed The Word.
You have sealed the journey in your body.
May your steps remember what your
soul already knows.

Choose the closing that best serves your setting. Silence is always an option.

Sealed in The Way

You have walked The Way.
You have breathed the Living Word
through bone and breath,
through stillness and surrender,
through rising and return.
What began in silence
has moved through form.
What was received in the breath
has been written into the body.
May the steps you took here
continue beyond this page.
May your feet remember the path of peace.
May your hands remain open to blessing.
May your heart stay tender and courageous.
May your breath always recognize the
Presence that gives it life.
May you carry The Way within you
not as a technique,
but as a manner of being.
When you rise, may you rise in truth.
When you bow, may you bow in trust.
When you stand, may you stand in love.
When you rest, may you rest in completeness.

Choose the closing that best serves your setting. Silence is always an option.

You are not unfinished.
You are not forgotten.
You are not outside the path.
You are held.
May The Aleph remind you to return to stillness.
May the letters continue to move within you.
May The Tav seal you in wholeness
not as an ending,
but as an Amen that carries forward.
"I am The Aleph and The Tav,
The Beginning and The End." *Revelation 22:13*
Go gently.
Walk faithfully.
Breathe deeply.
And when you forget,
may your body remember The Way.
Amen.

Choose the closing that best serves your setting. Silence is always an option.

For instructors to read.

Integration

Take a gentle breath here.
No need to change it, just notice it.
As we come to the close of this practice,
may the breath you've received stay with you, and may the movements you've offered continue to live quietly in your body.
May your feet remember steadiness.
May your hands remember openness.
May your heart remember safety and truth.
As you step back into your day,
may you carry The Way within you not as something to perform, but as something to walk in, gently and faithfully.
Go in peace.
Move in love.
Rest in what has been given.
Amen.

"Choose the closing that best serves your setting. Silence is always an option."

For instructors to read.

Hebrew Inflected Integration Blessing Aleph–Tav

Take one more gentle breath.
Let your body be at ease.
From Aleph the silent breath where all things begin to Tav, the seal of completion and truth you have walked The Way.

May the Ruach, the breath of life, remain with you. May what was opened be held with care, and may what was formed be carried forward in peace. As you rise from this place, may your steps be steady, your heart aligned, and your spirit at rest. You are sealed in love. You are grounded in truth. You are carried in life.
Aleph and Tav.
Beginning and Completion.
The Way is within you.
Amen.

(Optional teacher note — not spoken)
If desired, pause briefly after "Aleph and Tav"
to allow the room to breathe before saying "Amen."

"Choose the closing that best serves your setting. Silence is always an option."

Closing Blessing

May the breath you've taken remain with you, may the movement you've offered continue to guide you, and may The Way you walked here, settle softly into your body and your days. As you go, may your steps be steady, your heart open, and your spirit at rest sealed in love, grounded in truth, and carried forward in peace.

Amen.

#	Letter	Name	Hz	Chakra / Wheel	Ray	Color	Musical Note
1	א	Aleph	963	Crown (Keter)	Ray 1	White	B
2	ב	Bet	528	Heart	Ray 2	Green Yellow	E
3	ג	Gimel	528	Heart	Ray 4	Green	F
4	ד	Dalet	417	Sacral	Ray 2	Orange	D
5	ה	Hey	963 528	Third Eye → Heart	Ray 6 / 4	Indigo → Green	A → C
6	ו	Vav	369	Solar Plexus	Ray 2	Golden Yellow	E
7	ז	Zayin	693 / 963	Heart → Crown	Ray 7	Violet → White	F → B
8	ח	Chet	285	Heart	Ray 5	Green	B
9	ט	Tet	528	Heart	Ray 3	Rose / Pink	B
10	י	Yod	963	Crown	Ray 1	White-Violet	B

* Dual frequencies already appear in your Hey and Zayin entries and can be taught as "descending" or "ascending" variants.

#	Letter	Name	Hz	Chakra / Wheel	Ray	Color	Musical Note
11	כ	Kaf	432	Heart	Ray 4	Green	A
12	ל	Lamed	741	Throat	Ray 7	Violet	B
13	מ	Mem	417	Sacral	Ray 6	Blue	D
14	נ	Nun	639	Heart	Ray 4	Green	F
15	ס	Samekh	528	Heart	Ray 4	Green	F
16	ע	Ayin	639	Heart	Ray 5	Green	F
17	פ	Pei	731	Throat	Ray 5	Blue	G
18	צ	Tzadei	396	Root	Ray 1	Deep Red	F
19	ק	Qof	396	Root	Ray 1	Deep Red	G
20	ר	Resh	417	Heart	Ray 3	Green	F
21	ש	Shin	963	Crown	Ray 12	White	B
22	ת	Tav	396	Crown	Ray 1	White	B

Tenuat HaDerekh

Sacred Movement & Breath
with the Living Letters of Light

*A healing practice for body, soul, and spirit
rooted in Scripture, resonance, and faith.*

Chaplain Shawnna Schmidt

**Tenuat HaDerekh — Movement of The Way
A sacred practice of breath, embodiment, and return
© Chaplain Shawnna Schmidt**

Tenuat HaDerekh, Movement of The Way Series

HaDerekh. The Movement of The Way is a sacred, movement based practice rooted in breath, embodiment, and the Hebrew letters as living forms. Blending Scripture, contemplative movement, and embodied prayer, the series invites participants to encounter The Way not as doctrine alone, but as something lived through the body.

Across the series, readers are guided from awakening and remembrance, into integration in daily life, and eventually into the stewardship of sacred space for others. Each volume builds gently, honoring the body as a vessel of prayer, memory, and transformation.

HaDerekh is not a system to master, but a path to walk, slowly, reverently, and in rhythm with breath. The Way has always been near. It is learned not only by belief, but by movement.

Book I: HaDerekh: The Way Movement of the Living Letters
Book II: HaDerekh: A 30 day Alignment Practice
Book III: HaDerekh — The Path of Integration
Book IV: HaDerekh — The Way of the Teacher
Book V: HaDerekh — Letters of Fire
Sheva Ruach - The Sevenfold Way Of The Holy Spirit
HaDerekh Ruah - The Way of the Spirit

Tenuat HaDerekh — Movement of The Way
A sacred practice of breath, embodiment, and return
© Chaplain Shawnna Schmidt

Tenuat HaDerekh

Thirty Day Alignment

A 30 day Alignment practice for body, soul, and spirit rooted in Scripture, resonance, and faith.

Chaplain Shawnna Schmidt

Sheva Ruach

The Sevenfold Way of the Holy Spirit

*A Movement of The Way Immersion
in Awe, Alignment, and Love*

Chaplain Shawnna Schmidt

Books

By Chaplain Shawnna Schmidt

ALIGN WITH LOVE

The Little Leaf Who Remembered The Light

Devotional Series
Align With Love

- Awaken – A gentle stirring of the heart — inviting women to rise from spiritual slumber and rediscover the nearness of God's presence.
- Arise – A call to step forward with courage, truth, and purpose, standing firmly in the identity Heaven has spoken over you.
- Abide – A devotional of rest and rootedness — learning to dwell in God's love, peace, and steadying rhythm of grace.
- Anointed – A blessing-filled journey that reminds women of the oil, favor, and divine purpose poured over their lives since the beginning.

Series Summary:
A four-part devotional path offering 53 weeks of inspiration, Scripture, healing reflection, and alignment with Love.

Be, A Story of Orgin

A contemplative journey back to the beginning — where Light, Breath, and the Creator's Voice shaped all things. A poetic exploration of who we are, where we come from, and the divine resonance written into every soul.

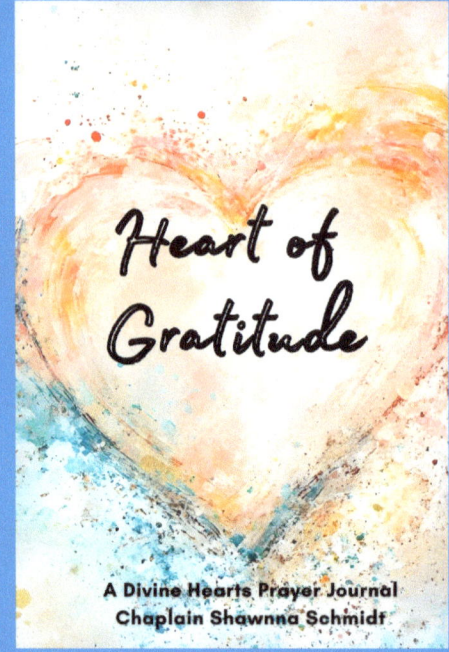

Heart of Gratitude

52-Week Journal

A year of cultivating beauty, awareness, and thankfulness — where creativity and reflection open the heart to joy, hope, and deeper connection with God.

HaShem

Healing Through The Names of God

A sacred encounter with the Holy One through His revealed Names — exploring their frequencies, meanings, and the healing they release into body, soul, and spirit.

COMING SOON

Frequency Doula

A contemplative journey back to the beginning — where Light, Breath, and the Creator's Voice shaped all things. A poetic exploration of who we are, where we come from, and the divine resonance written into every soul.

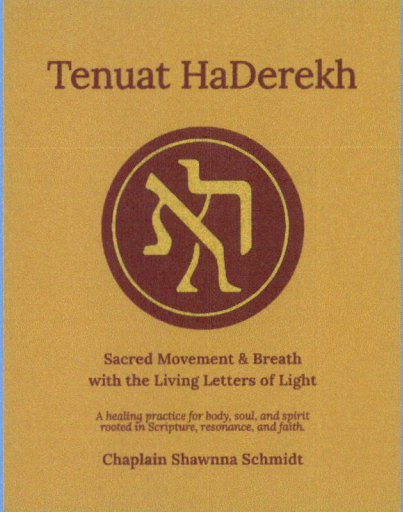

Movement of the Way

Where movement meets prayer, and awareness becomes worship.
Movement of the Way invites you into a rhythm of embodied faith — cultivating gratitude, presence, and spiritual alignment through weekly reflections and soul-tending practices. connection with God.

First Light

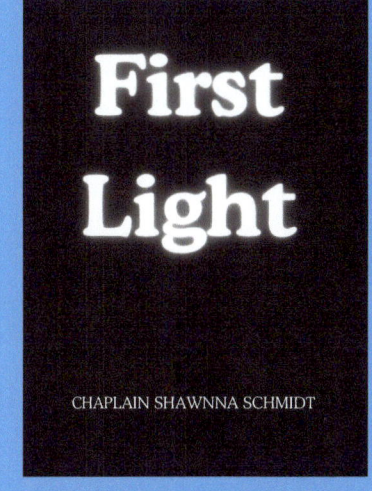

More than a study, First Light is a remembrance a return to the sacred truth that we were formed in Light, made to carry Light, and forever guided by the Light that spoke the world into being.
A timeless resource for seekers, teachers, and anyone longing to understand the radiance at the beginning of every story and the Light that still leads us on.

Inspired Messenger

Chaplain Shawnna Schmidt

Chaplain Shawnna Schmidt is a faith-rooted teacher, chaplain, and embodied-prayer guide whose work bridges Scripture, breath, and the living wisdom of the body. She is the founder of Movement of The Way (Tenuat HaDerekh,) a sacred movement practice rooted in the Hebrew Scriptures, the Messianic path of Yeshua, and the ancient understanding that faith is something we walk, not merely believe.

Drawing from Hebraic thought, embodied worship, nervous-system awareness, and a lifetime of pastoral care, Shawnna teaches that the body is not separate from prayer, it is the vessel through which prayer becomes lived. Her work gently restores connection between Body, Soul, and Spirit through movement, breath, Scripture, and stillness.

Shaped by motherhood, caregiving, resilience, and wonder, her calling has been refined through both joy and trial. She writes and teaches for those who love God deeply yet long to feel grounded, safe, and at home in their bodies again.
Each book in the HaDerekh series is offered not as instruction alone, but as invitation—an unfolding walk back to the ancient path, where the Word becomes flesh once more, and the body remembers how to say yes.

HaDerekh — The Way
Movement of the Living Letters

HaDerekh, The Way is a breath-led, body-based spiritual practice rooted in the Hebrew letters as living forms. It invites readers into embodied prayer through gentle movement, sacred posture, and attentive breath. Not as performance, but as presence.

Drawing from Scripture, Hebrew thought, and the embodied ministry of Yeshua, this book reclaims the body as a sacred vessel, a place where prayer is lived, not merely spoken. Each letter becomes an invitation to listen, align, and move with intention, allowing faith to be carried not only in belief, but in the body itself.

Designed for personal devotion, group practice, and teaching settings, HaDerekh offers adaptive postures, theological reflection, and contemplative guidance accessible to all bodies and abilities.

Silence is honored. Stillness is welcomed. Movement becomes a form of remembering. This book is not meant to be rushed. It is meant to be walked. Because before prayer had words, it had breath. And the body already knows the way.

www.ingramcontent.com/pod-product-compliance
Lightning Source LLC
Chambersburg PA
CBHW041518220426
43667CB00002B/31